AT THE GATES
HAZEM FAHMY

This is a work of fiction. All names, characters, places, and incidents are a product of the author's imagination. Any resemblance to real events or persons, living or dead, is entirely coincidental.

Published by Akashic Books
©2023 Hazem Fahmy
ISBN: 978-1-63614-131-2

All rights reserved
Printed in China
First printing

Akashic Books
Brooklyn, New York
Twitter, Facebook, Instagram: AkashicBooks
E-mail: info@akashicbooks.com
Website: www.akashicbooks.com

African Poetry Book Fund
Prairie Schooner
University of Nebraska
110 Andrews Hall
Lincoln, Nebraska 68588

TABLE OF CONTENTS

Preface by Danusha Laméris 5

Interrogation of Alternate Time Line 7
The Drowned Rise from the Mediterranean 9
'Ars (عرص) Poetica 12
In Which I Leave Behind My Passport 14
Moses 16
At the Gates, Gibril Asks Me Where I Come From 17
At the Gates, Mikhail Makes Me a Feast of Rain and Dirt 21
Ahha (اها) Poetica 24
Surur Teaches Me How to Say Ahha (اها) 26
Abdel Halim Performs a Private Concert for My Mother 28
Me and Edward Draw a Map in English 30
Ars Poetica 34

Notes 36
Glossary of Arabic Terms and Phrases 38

PREFACE
by Danusha Laméris

If it's true that we read to cover distances, then how much greater a pleasure to read that which takes us on a journey of both inner and outer terrain. Hazem Fahmy, emerging Egyptian poet, is an experienced guide as he carries us gracefully through such landscapes. These poems bow to the risk of speech itself, born of a world in which words are perilous, and the lives of those who dare to speak, endangered. There is much music in these lines, and the pleasure of the words and speaking them has been made a sacrament. When I arrive at the gates of these poems I feel the shudder of such rhythms: "I was a sleeping city. / Once, I played my oud / for the sea and he arched / his soft back; called me / beautiful, and whole." ("The Drowned Rise from the Mediterranean")

These lines cover oceans and deserts. They cover history, the territory of the holy, distance from home and from country, distance from the mother tongue. We feel the longing in that distance, and yet, in the searching, there is also finding. "I've come this far / already," the speaker reminds himself. This is why we read poetry: to know what it is to survive. There is earned wisdom here: "I speak every name / God ever gave me," Fahmy tells us, and we are invited to remember the names we, too, were given. ("Self-Portrait as Moses")

Here, grief is its own gorgeous landscape; a world in which even the smallest blossom in the parched soil is cause to bend down and kiss the earth in praise. Here, "mangled text" becomes a poem, and "Joy," Fahmy tells us, "is an imperfect sentence" ("Surur Teaches Me How to Say Ahha [اها]"). It's that pull toward life that is most evident in the enfolding of *At the Gates*. The singing not *because of*, but *in spite of*.

I admire the way these poems allow Fahmy's speaker to step into alternate versions of his story:

> In another life, what must be said
> here is but fairytale, ghost stories
> for the rowdy children. Kanafani would live
> in Acre, Baldwin would die
> in Harlem, neither knowing the taste
> of exile. I would write of bees
> and clocks. I would not need men's solemn
> crooning to put me
> to sleep. I would not mourn
> the dead.
>
> ("Interrogation of Alternate Time Line")

And yet, he reckons with life as it is, as it has been, and makes of it a distinct and memorable music.

In the end, it's the sheer lyric power and beauty of the lines themselves that carry us home. This is language that is hard won, that vibrates, not only within the lines, but underneath them. It's the thing that cannot be taught, the thing that brings us, inexplicably, back to some poets and not others. Fahmy is a poet I expect to return to, and who I hope continues to return to us.

In the final poem, speaking for those who have bent themselves to fit the shape of English, he uses the familiar, unasked for language and contorts it into a new shape of beauty: "We / alchemy the tongue. We epic / rhetoric, revive dead rivers with / every word reclaimed." ("Me and Edward Draw a Map in English")

INTERROGATION OF ALTERNATE TIME LINE

On a dusty rooftop in Giza, I tell Imam,
in another life, he and Hugh would have been
the best of friends. I picture Hugh, taking him
by the arm down the corniche
or the Cape, the cool night air refusing
silence. I hear their strings and tubes cutting through
beaming crowds in Imbaba and Soweto. Miriam
is serenading an open sea, clicking to the wind
by el-Montazah. I see Biko
and Negm, side by side, in a crowded auditorium,
a whole generation huddled
around their voices. This is to say, in another
life, revolution would be but
abstract. Biko would be a doctor,
perhaps in Durban. There would be no trains
for Hugh to sing of, save for those
that would bring him back to his loved
ones, safely. Negm would only be known
for love poems. What more
could one ask for? Let us not cheer
for those who would rather die
as soldiers when there is no
war. My whole life I have envied
the kind of thirst for music
that can be quenched by
Elvis and Sinatra. I have prayed
nightly for those I have idolized
to find a good night's sleep
before deadly fame. What good is poetry

if it kills the poet? In another life, what must be said
here is but fairy tale, ghost stories
for the rowdy children. Kanafani would live
in Acre, Baldwin would die
in Harlem, neither knowing the taste
of exile. I would write of bees
and clocks. I would not need men's solemn
crooning to put me
to sleep. I would not mourn
the dead.

THE DROWNED RISE FROM THE MEDITERRANEAN

1

حرام تنسوني بالمرة

Before I board the plane, I ask
for forgiveness. I found
my body drifting

in the Atlantic, fingers broken
off, nails chipped, lost to the depths.
I found my body in a faraway

land and it was a gruesome
sight—hair burning,
a cloud of smoke chasing

an endless horizon.
I was a sleeping city.
Once, I played my oud

for the sea and he arched
his soft back; called me
beautiful, and whole:

a crimson rose in a blood-
less spring.

2

أنا والله كنت مفكّرتك برّات البلاد

How dare I call another
soil any syllable like
home? Once, I was lied to; told

my body was safe(r) here,
and I believed the devil—looked
back at the river that raised me in

shame, head bowed. Now, I search
for any vessel
that will take me.

3

يا هوا دخل الهوا خدني على بلادي

In my dreams, I see him stand,
fully grown. Death,
a bitter illusion. Here,

he stands,
arms open wide, welcoming
all of us *home*. Here, he scoffs

when I show him my passport,
rips apart the fragile thing
in one motion. I am sorry: force

of habit, والله. He says:
I know, حبيبي. And someday
you will, too.

'ARS (عرص) POETICA

Let us assume Marx was an incomplete
man: a half-spilled bottle of ink. In this way,
we liberate the mouth, summon back
a voice that has made a home out of rust:

إلخ، إلخ، إالخ

والله

I never needed a beard to save me,
certainly not a mustache. So let us
regroup and assume that Nasser, too, was
an incomplete man: heart no bigger than
a barracks.

يابني، مصر أم الدنيا

Would you give your mama sloppy seconds?
A jammed rifle? Go buy your mama
a tank, an air force. Mama my معلم

طيارة شوية عليها

my mama knows her history, needed
neither a man in uniform nor his
cowardly bullets. After prayer we will break
bread and assume that Guevara,
too, was an incomplete man: a face of fire
extinguished too early to light

anything proper here. Don't take that poster down
unless you want to, we all make do with what little
space we get: look what our fathers built with
bleeding hands. Sooner or later you will
traverse this majestic travesty. Don't cry
for bleached pharaohs, we still have the real
deal, dirt cheap.

أوكازيون غير كده ما فيش

Ramses had chubby knees, I saw myself.

التفتكره ما بيفتكرش

What do you know of harvests? Never reap
what a foreigner has sowed unless they
did it with open palms, a face toward
the sky. If you've ever seen a field of wheat,
you know Cromer was a complete white
man, not strictly, but professionally; a polished medal
drenched in rain, a truly exquisite
shine. Seek out that metal which does
the same for you. We all want to be
remembered, either in stone or by name—hence the
oath
we swear to paper, hence the incompleteness of life
with incomplete papers, hence people
are so ungrateful

والله

Someday we will forget the sun.

IN WHICH I LEAVE BEHIND MY PASSPORT

green as spring, mint leaves swirling
in dark: red, green, black. I want
no flags in my tea. No filth
in my teeth.

يا بدوي

swirl me around, I want to dance
with my country. Give her a dress,
whatever she likes,
whatever fits or doesn't.

أنا لا أتمنيت
ولا قلت
يا ريت

but I will come back with all
the paper possible, and we
will fold every story
we've ever needed, hang them

like فوانيس on a cold
Ramadan night. If I am to die
tomorrow, let my body not
make the dirt

sigh. If I die tomorrow,
let my body make
a *home* of the dirt that held
my *home*. Before I die

tomorrow, let my *home* be
a polished temple. Let someone
pray there
in peace.

MOSES

I walk through deserts, searching
for God and country, or at least
a promise. No "son" loves

this moment, the aching back
turned on everything ever
known. I plead for the sand

to deliver me. And it sighs.
For all the sins it counts.
Day in and day out, I watch

the sun sink, read my blessings
on calloused palms. Every crack
whispers gratitude. I've come this far

already. There are
no mirages where I am heading.
I speak every name

God ever gave me, hold them
close like my children at night
by fire. I see blood every-

where, but this is still a land
without wolves, littered with burnt
flags. I do not let myself

forget that.

AT THE GATES, GIBRIL ASKS ME WHERE I COME FROM

He says: the beginning. I say:

> The 10th millennium Before Christ,
> hunter-gatherers up the Nile terraces replaced
> by a grinding culture. Then, around 8000 BC,
> tribal peoples migrated to the Nile basin where they developed
> a centralized society.

But this is not enough, so
I say:

> The English name *Egypt* is derived
> from the Ancient Greek *Aígyptos* (Αἴγυπτος), through the Middle
> French *Egypte* and the Latin *Aegyptus*. *Misr*
> (or as it is pronounced in Egyptian Arabic, مَصر) however,
> comes from Classic Quranic Arabic and remains
> the modern official name of Egypt.
>
> The name is of Semitic origin, cognate
> with other Semitic words for Egypt. For example:
> the Hebrew *Mitzráyim* (מִצְרַיִם).

Still, this is not enough, so
I say:

> After the time of Yusuf, Musa was born
> into a family of Israelites living in Egypt after
> the Pharaoh had enslaved the Israelites after his dream
> of a fire coming straight from Jerusalem, burning all
> in his kingdom except the Israelites.

In a few millennia, in the year 42 anno
Domini, the first church is established in Egypt, by Morkos
the Evangelist. Soon, the patriarchate of Alexandria becomes
one of the centers through which Christianity spreads.

Six hundred years later, Amr ibn al-'As left for Egypt
in December 639 AD with a force of four thousand troops.
'Umar, thinking it foolish to conquer such a large
country with a mere force of four thousand, wrote a letter
to Amr commanding him to come back. Amr didn't
heed the letter and went on to capture all of Egypt
by 642 AD.

He says:

I have heard all this before.

I say:

July '56, Egypt nationalized the Suez
Canal Company, closing the canal to Israeli
shipping. Israel responds by invading the Sinai
Peninsula with British and French support.

During the Suez Crisis, Israel captured Gaza
and Sinai, but the US and the UN soon pressured
it into a ceasefire, so Israel acquiesces to a withdrawal
from Egyptian territory and Egypt agreed to allow
freedom of navigation in the region.

> Eleven years later, Israel would claim this freedom
> as justification for the so-called Six Day War, in which all
> of historic Palestine, Sinai, and the Golan were occupied
> by Israel. Gamal Abdel Nasser dies before Sinai is free.

He says:

> Not every story has to
> be written in bullets.

I say:

> Jama'at al-Tawhid wal-Jihad was founded in '99
> in Iraq, where it pledged its allegiance to al-Qaeda
> and joined the insurgency following the invasion
> of Western forces. About fifteen years later, the group
> proclaimed itself a worldwide caliphate and began
> to refer to itself as the Islamic State (الدولة الإسلامية) or IS

.
He takes my hand, tells me:

> سمي الشيطان بإسمه

I say:

> The khawal (خول, plural khawalat, similar to the Turkish,
> köçek), a traditional Egyptian "male" dancer, cross-
> dressed, feminine attire, popular up until the
> late-eighteenth, early-nineteenth centuries. The tradition
> of gender-bending performers in Arabia can be traced
> back to pre-Islamic times, like in Egypt, where they gained

prominence, after Muhammad Ali banned female dancers, who were replaced by khawalat, who were found seductive. The practice wasn't banned until the twenties. Now, a khawal is the closest Egyptian Arabic has to "fag."

He says:

I asked for a name.

I say:

A man I once trusted reached under my covers and my father blames his hands for the death of my manhood.

He says:

إحمل الصخر فوق الجبل وإرميه

I say:

A culture of hunters replaced the Nile, developed a centralized English via French. *Egypte. Aegyptus. Misr. Mitzráyim.* Semitic Musa. Enslaved dream. Fire from Jerusalem. Everything kingdom, except anno Domini. Morkos centers six hundred years. Amr left. 'Umar wrote. Nationalized the company, invaded Sinai, Gaza. Israel agreed. Freedom of navigation. Iraq. Caliphate. Khawal. Köçek. Tradition. Native Arabia, traced centuries. Muhammad Ali banned. Seductive years. Egyptian faggot. Trust. Reach. Manhood.

He lets my hand go, opens the gates wide.

AT THE GATES, MIKHAIL MAKES ME A FEAST OF RAIN AND DIRT

    For which I'm truly grateful.
I've spent a lifetime dreaming
       of cities wide enough
                to hold me. I have feared open
                  roads; the seduction of
             the unfathomable. All my life

I have prayed for a soil
    unburdened by time, say an
Eden of a nap. And yet,
               I sit before him alone.
            He asks me about my kin
               and country. I say: I am

sorry if I ever spoke
    out of a mouth that was not
mine. I say "we" and hope that means
            something. I don't pretend
               to know where "we" live. If there
          is a place for "us" I have

    known it only by name, but
never map. I have looked for "us"
    on the highway, only
            found sirens, restless screeching;
               choir of dust, shriveled lotus
           by an empty bank. Maybe

"we" are all just in love with
    scorched temples, dead languages.
Every dry river has a lake

                              for a mother, and I am tired
                           of the violence of water;
                              how it holds the still land

with its ego. Somewhere,
     there's history without
burden. There is an "us" I don't have

                    to wash of blood and
                              kerosene. Cut off my tongue
                    if I claim I know what it

     looks like, but hear me when
I say it does not smell
     like gated flowers, or stale fear

                         underneath a thick blanket.
                              I know I too am guilty
                         of this legacy. I have praised

the dirt I have spat on
     only when it grows
what I ask of it. I've dug a grave

                         for every nightingale
                    who sang too loud. And for that you
                         can call my mouth rotten, but

never rested الحمد لله
     Insomnia's the only
vocab my city ever

                    gave me, and I speak it well,
                         let it overflow from my open
                    mouth unto the tired

    earth. I know "we" have all grown
weary from the taste of rust,
    how its brittle trauma makes

                      a *home* out of our teeth. But
                        find me a history that
                  has ever undone "us" and

I will go to bed tonight
    unfazed by the summer. He
says: it is foolish to fear

                    the dark. I say: God gifts us
            the night, and for that I am
                  eternally grateful. There

were days when I wished myself
    small enough to die
in the flame of a lantern, but I

                have settled for that music
                    which shakes the stillness. I have
            mocked martyrdom's allure, I am

    weak یا ربی I was
never anything like Bilal or Omar.
    Forgive me my timid jaw,

                my quiet hands. They only
                want to build.

AHHA (اهّا) POETICA

The poem is the quest for the scream,
that knife which cuts the night
crimson, leads the dirt in song,
marks holy territory with blood. This poem isn't
about blood, but it might as well be.
Let's pump preposterously. Pretend
it's oil, and you'll find
it. Once, a whole nation went
to war for an orgasm: why
should we settle for less? This poem is the body, so it
too is searching for a good
time, requited with a roar;
the river that greets the sea
with a gentle shiver. Say please
and thank you. Say أقسم بالله.
This body dance truth, retained
scripture. Yes, I read (for) pleasure;
a subtle ecstasy, but the breath is still
tested. لا حول و لا قوة إلا بالله Do you know
what that means? Why shouldn't God
smile down upon my sweat? What is love
without labor? The body demands
the scream. I live for the stolen
breath, brought back. Exhale.
اها What do you think
Hind Rostom did in that barn? The train
screeched. I know the moan is
our inheritance. Bring it back
soft and steady; the heavy breath

before dawn—not of waiting. A watched street
never marches. Bring back the protest.
Bring it here in my throat, in my chest.
Inhale. اها Say اها. Say it tender. Say
it loud. Behold a revived
grammar: a thousand اهاs I lay
upon you. Oh اها my
اها: give me اها or give me
اها. My one regret is that
I have but one اها to اها my اها.
Oh, see can you اها? If not now,
then tomorrow. Let the morning
bring you.
اها

SURUR TEACHES ME HOW TO SAY AHHA (احا)

And mean it; a screech of joy
so sharp makes a كافر bow.

Here, the mangled text that will
become a poem—loose language—

blueprint for a reckoning.
Fuck a philology. Joy

is the imperfect sentence.
Syntax gone wrong and proudly:

burnt dish I eat anyway,
smiling. I say: الحمد لله and mean

it, just as much. I have always
wanted to grow up

to be wind; impermanent,
yet ever present—paired

with a sunset to die for. The right
gust at the right time was all

Mama ever needed
to see a sign from God. What

is winter to the breeze? A flood
to the sea? Once, I was but

a drop in still water,
and I have made my peace

with that. What is more احلى than this
moment? I make Naguib قهوة,

darker than earth, and it lasts
the whole day. He reads my cup,

says he sees great احلى in my
future. I say: I have kept

the احلى safe under
my tongue where no uninvited

hand may snatch it at night. This
is how we've survived.

ABDEL HALIM PERFORMS A PRIVATE CONCERT FOR MY MOTHER

Once, in a stolen land that wanted
my name dead, I knew

nothing of drums and strings. Once,
I could not wake if Imam

did not bring the sun to my
cursed bed. If nothing else, I listened

carefully, heard Abdel Wahab
trick their colonial

ass. This is the rhythm of unflinching,
the sea as still

as night—we like it that way.
Here, I ask Mama again

what she needs but a radio
and she still says: batteries,

and well-pressed clothes for my child—
just so we look good when we cry

to Om Kalthoum. Once,
in a stolen land that wished

my tongue in the ocean, I could
not explain what it meant to cry

without tragedy. Now,
I hold Mama's hand as we weep

to his crooning. I raise
my hand; a request—سواح.

He smiles and asks me: for what?
We are here now, حبيبي

Then for old time's sake, I plead,
for chorus of memory,

percussion as cool as dew.
And so me and Mama cry

with Abdel Halim, as we
did with Fairuz, and every

song that brought the breath back to
an empty chest. Once, I spent

a lifetime incapable
of drawing a map *home*, but

والله

I have always known what it
sounds like.

ME AND EDWARD DRAW A MAP IN ENGLISH

But first, I say: يا عمي   I have never been taught a geography
                                    unmarked by cataclysm,   all
islands seem
to be drowning.   He frowns, grunts a sweet sound
                            only a عمو second to no man but
                        Baba can muster. Asks: isn't that what their vile
mouths
have always wanted? يابنى every dawn
is a gift.   Who are we without open arms?
                              I know too well what it is to dream
                              without rest. I have asked for nothing
                        but hair of thick night, brushed
                    across a brown brow, clear;
a beckoning horizon,
all my children need to know
that day is always coming,
                              the light is already here.
يا سلام

                              What has the world made of you?
I confess: an apparition in transit; eyes like
                    scarabs, small desert things, as silly
                as they are pretty, can be crushed if
            need be.
I had a mouth of dry sea, an empty
landscape, miles of antiques
poking out of the sand. I had the teeth
of a dull blade, of recession and wasted aid.
I had the neck of lamb, soft when silenced.

                              Children gathered to watch how
                    kitchen knives made a budding rose
               of it. I had a chest of bronze, as in
          the age, as in
a language bowing to a foreigner's name.
I had   the heart of a stallion shipped as far
                         as possible from the land that birthed
               him. I had
the gut of the calm after
the storm has been forgotten, after
we turn around the boats, let sand and sea
make a *home* out of our brethren's still bodies.
I had   an arm of rubber, flexible to a fault. Knees of
gelatin—   there was nothing halal about this. My feet were a
force to be laughed at,   but also lined up; given
direction
when needed.   *And now that you have walked here*, he asks,
*what will you make
of the morning?*   *What is a land unburdened by
                blood?* I say: I want a here
we craft
with our hands;   bring your folk—tell them to bring
               their folk, all folk who've inherited
          the taste of steel,   and all folk who vow to
     spit it out. We will
meet under an open sky.
Bring your bread, your rice,
your chicken. I know no greater love
than the warm hand after the full belly,
or a wave of music washing over
a gyrating body, the ecstasy
of jiving to the earth.

*And what of the weight
of language*, he interrupts,
how does the body learn to   carry that which once tried to break
                                           us.

Mourn a century. I know
he knows the answer,
nonetheless, I say: I long to lock arms with all y'all, my
                             beoble;
all my beobles, come: let us rudely interrupt our own
                             English. I don't need you to explain
                     what that word means.   I've left all screens in a
faraway world.
Put your throat against mine. Let us vibrate
viciously,   accentuate all accented syllables. My whole
life I waited for a spring
of strings and now   this music is the only kind of
                       language I need. Once, I cursed the
              prick of that tongue that could not
       say my name. Here,
I find enough forgiveness to bury
the violence of this English. Here,   I can say: praise
English,   and you know I mean *our* English,
as spoken by Mama and Baba, broken
and rebuilt by the b's of my teita: do you hear
how her bronunciation is boetry
in and of itself?   English—reborn, glowing as
                 accents, vernaculars, pidgins,
           creoles—
baptized in all the glory weak hands
once tried to snatch from us—all of us—
who never asked for this language, but have   bent to fit our bodies just the same. We

32

  alchemy the tongue. We epic
rhetoric, revive dead rivers with   every word reclaimed. We summon the rain
with our throats. يا شعوبي
At last here comes   a train we don't need to fear. Screech
    serenades the night, like
Hugh's trumpet. Behold,   a river of dark wine without sin, borders
nothing but a deranged
dying man's fever dream. A song
we stop listening to.   Edward smiles. He takes me by the
    shoulder:

    Drink up. Drink whole. We've earned a wide
    world we will never need to apologize for.

ARS POETICA

بإسم الله

Like everything, begin at the river,
flood the sea. Here, a land claimed
beneath a quiet moon, his face unshaven. With lust
for light burn Homer, Aristotle, and Virgil. If horses
gallop here they neigh symphonies: hoodlums'
howls. 'Lectro-Sha3bi, max volume.

الدنيا مش مرجيحة
الدنيا متناكة

We can't speak of mothers before burying
Hypatia and Cleopatra. Time is of the essence
so let this be the time for Mariam,
not Mary, Scheherazade—Zeinab
if available. We will not ask for that
which cannot be given, unless it be hiding
out in museums that charge euros
or dollars. That's our shit. Imam said so
long ago. Not objectively,
but permanently. So let's Edward Said
motherfuckers, make occidentals out of con-
tinentals. I don't care for English lest it be blood-
stained
and broken. Dictate that dialect. Assert
your accent. Smoke cigs
like Youssef Chahine. Flick it on film reels.
We reject celluloid unless we have projectors.
Oum Kalthoum will do fine on Spotify.
Before you sleep say good night.
Today, Zaghloul. Tomorrow whoever.

I could be wrong about Zaghloul. We've zig-
zagged here before.

ده إنجليزى؟

طب ده صوت؟

I don't know. I know the sound of Cairo.
I know how the sea cries. Find your Darwish.
I don't care which. Find the kind of song
that takes you there:

خذني على بلادي

I don't care where, what, or who.

الأسمراني

What about?

عملة أى الغربة فيه

Ask again.

طمنوني

and again and again and again and
again and just when you're done: again.

NOTES

Mentions of Imam and Negm throughout the manuscript are references to the leftist Egyptian folk duo, Sheikh Imam Eissa and Ahmed Fouad Negm.

In "Interrogation of Alternate Time Line," Hugh and Miriam refer to the South African musicians Hugh Masekela and Miriam Makeba, while Biko refers to the socialist organizer and thinker Steve Biko. In their own ways, each of them contributed immeasurably to the heroic struggle against apartheid, and Biko gave his life for it in 1977. The mention of trains is a reference to Masekela's song "Stimela." Kanafani refers to the Palestinian communist writer and organizer, Ghassan Kanafani, who was assassinated by the apartheid regime that colonized his land.

"The Drowned Rise from the Mediterranean" is written after Hanif Abdurraqib and uses lyrics from the Sayed Darwish song, popularized by Fairuz, "Zorouny Kol Sana Marah / Visit Me Once a Year," and the Fairuz songs "Keifak / How Are You," and "Nasam Alayna el-Hawa / The Breeze Blew Upon Us."

In "'Ars (عرص) Poetica" Nasser refers to the second Egyptian President Gamal Abdel Nasser. This poem satirically uses a lyric from the Saad Lamjarred song "L'ma'lem / You Are the Boss." Cromer refers to Everly Baring, the first colonial administrator of the British occupation of Egypt in the late 19th century.

"In Which I Leave Behind My Passport" uses lyrics from the Sheikh Imam songs, "Ana el-Adeeb el-Odabaty / I Am the Poetic Poet" and "Ana Atoub 'an Hobak / How Can I Let Go of Your Love."

In "At the Gates, Gibril Asks Me Where I Come From," Gibril is the mainstream Egyptian pronunciation of Gabriel, here referring to the archangel. The poem uses lyrics from the Mashrou' Leila songs, "3 Minutes" and "Wa Nueid / And We Repeat."

In "At the Gates, Mikhail Makes Me a Feast of Rain and Dirt," Mikhail is the Arabic pronunciation of Michael, here referring to the archangel. Bilal and Omar here refer to Bilal ibn Rabah and 'Umar ibn-al-Khattab, two of the closest companions of the Prophet Muhammad.

In "Ahha (اها) Poetica," the mention of Hind Rostom in the barn is a reference to the 1958 Youssef Chahine film, *Bab el-Hadid / Cairo Station*.

In "Surur Teaches Me How to Say Ahha (اها)," Surur refers to the radical Egyptian poet Naguib Surur.

"Abdel Halim Performs a Private Concert for My Mother" is written after Safia Elhillo. Abdel Halim Hafez, Mohamed Abdel Wahab, and Oum Kalthoum are widely considered to be three of the most important figures in 20th century Egyptian and Arabophone music.

In "Me and Edward Draw a Map in English" Edward refers to the late Palestinian American scholar Edward Said.

Electro-Sha'bi (spelled 'Lectro-Sha3bi in "Ars Poetica") is a term for various hybrid genres of modern Egyptian music. This poem references a lyric from the Amr el-Said song "el-Donya Zay el-Morgeha / Life Is like a Swing." Zaghloul refers to the anti-British Egyptian revolutionary Saad Zaghloul. The poem uses lyrics from the Fairuz song "Nasam Alayna el-Hawa / The Breeze Blew Upon Us" and the Abdel Halim Hafez song "Sawah / Tourist."

GLOSSARY OF ARABIC TERMS AND PHRASES

el-Montazah	a historic park in Alexandria
حرام تنسوني بالمرة	God forbid, don't forget me all at once
أنا والله كنت مفكّرتك برّات البلاد	I swear, I thought you'd left the country
يا هوا دخل الهوا خدني على بلادي	O, breeze, for the sake of love, take me home
أقسم بالله / والله	I swear
حبيبي	My beloved
عرص	Bastard
إلخ، إلخ، إالخ	Etc.
يابني، مصر أم الدنيا	My child, Egypt is the mother of the world
معلم	Boss / elder
طيارة شوية عليها	A plane is cheap for her
أوكازيون غير كده ما فيش	Discount, unlike any other
التفتكره ما بيفتكرش	He you remember will forget you
أنا لا أتمنيت ولا قلت يا ريت	I never wished for anything but you
فوانيس	Lanterns
سمي الشيطان باسمه	Call the devil by his name
إحمل الصخر فوق الجبل وإرميه	Carry the rock over the mountain and throw it
الحمد لله	Thank god
احا	Vulgar colloquial Egyptian expletive, allegedly referring to the sound of an orgasm
لا حول و لا قوة إلا بالله	There is no power, but from god
كافر	Heretic

قهوة	Coffee
سواح	Tourist, with the implication of being somewhat lost. Also the title of a popular Abdel Halim song.
عمو / يا عمي	O, uncle
يابنى	My child
يا سلام	Oh, my
يا شعوبي	My peoples
الدنيا مش مرجيحة	The world is unlike a swing
الدنيا متناكة	The world is fucked
ده إنجليزي؟	Is this English?
طب ده صوت؟	Is this even a voice?
خذني على بلادي	Take me to my country
عملة أى الغربة فيه	What has being away done to him?
طمنوني	Let me know / alleviate my anxiety

I am indebted and grateful to the editors of the following journals for giving earlier versions of these poems a home. Much thanks to everyone at: *Ambit,* the *Boston Review, Five:2:One, Foglifter, The Margins, Poem-a-Day, the Scores,* and *Tinderbox.*